D1532092

Funny FiLL-IN
MY WILD WEST ADVENTURE

NATIONAL GEOGRAPHIC SOCIETY
WASHINGTON, D.C.

How to Play Funny Fill-In!

Love to create amazing stories? Good, because this one stars YOU. Get ready to laugh with all your friends—you can play with as many people as you want! Make sure to keep this book on your shelf. You'll want to read it again and again!

Are You Ready to Laugh?

- One person picks a story—you can start at the beginning, the middle, or the end of the book.

- Ask a friend to call out a word that the space asks for—noun, verb, or something else—and write it in the blank space. If there's more than one player, ask the next person to say a word. Extra points for creativity!

- When all the spaces are filled in, you have your very own Funny Fill-In. Read it out loud for a laugh.

- Want to play by yourself? Just fold over the page and use the cardboard insert at the back as a writing pad. Fill in the blank parts of speech list, and copy your answers into the story.

Make sure you check out the amazing **Fun Facts** that appear on every page!

Parts of Speech

To play the game, you'll need to know how to form sentences. This list with examples of the parts of speech and other terms will help you get started:

Noun: The name of a person, place, thing, or idea
Examples: tree, mouth, creature
*The **ocean** is full of colorful **fish**.*

Adjective: A word that describes a noun or pronoun
Examples: green, lazy, friendly
*My **silly** dog won't stop laughing!*

Verb: An action word. In the present tense, a verb often ends in –s or –ing. If the space asks for past tense, changing the vowel or adding a –d or –ed to the end usually will set the sentence in the past.
Examples: swim, hide, plays, running (present tense); biked, rode, jumped (past tense)
*The giraffe **skips** across the savanna.*
*The flower **opened** after the rain.*

Adverb: A word that describes a verb and usually ends in –ly
Examples: quickly, lazily, soundlessly
*Kelley **greedily** ate all the carrots.*

Plural: More than one
Examples: mice, telephones, wrenches
*Why are all the **doors** closing?*

Silly Word or Exclamation: A funny sound, a made-up word, a word you think is totally weird, or a noise someone or something might make
Examples: Ouch! No way! Foozleduzzle! Yikes!
*"**Darn!**" shouted Jim. "These cupcakes are sour!"*

Specific Words: There are many more ways to make your story hilarious. When asked for something like a number, animal, or body part, write in something you think is especially funny.

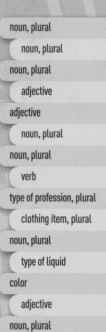

- noun, plural
- noun, plural
- noun, plural
- adjective
- adjective
- noun, plural
- noun, plural
- verb
- type of profession, plural
- clothing item, plural
- noun, plural
- type of liquid
- color
- adjective
- noun, plural

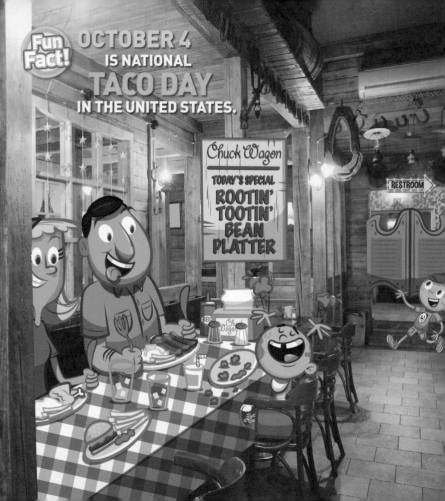

Door to the Past

Mmm! Mom and Dad are taking me out for Tex-Mex at the Chuck Wagon restaurant for my birthday.

I love _____ piled high and covered in cheesy _____ . I've been reading about the
    noun, plural   noun, plural

Wild West, a land without _____ , where _____ cowboys and _____
                       noun, plural   adjective   adjective

cowgirls roamed the _____ , looking for _____ . While we _____ , we're
                   noun, plural   noun, plural   verb

entertained by _____ wearing Western-style _____ and singing
    type of profession, plural   clothing item, plural

country and western songs while playing _____ . After gulping down lots of _____ ,
                            noun, plural   type of liquid

I have to visit the bathroom. But as I pass through the saloon doors, I suddenly see _____ skies,
                                                               color

_____ plains as far as the eye can see, and cowboys riding _____ . I'm back in the
 adjective   noun, plural

Wild West!

THE FIRST **COWBOYS** WERE THE **VAQUEROS**—MEN WHO WORKED ON **CATTLE RANCHES** IN MEXICO.

- sound ending in –ing
  - name of a group of animals
- large number
  - adjective
- noun
  - noun, plural
- verb ending in –ing
  - verb ending in –ing
- silly word
  - adjective
- color
  - clothing item
- adjective
  - nickname
- verb
  - noun

Cowboy Calling

I hear lots of _____ (sound ending in –ing) . Then I see them! I'm surrounded by a(n) _____ (name of a group of animals)

of cattle. There must be _____ (large number) of them! Some are covered in _____ (adjective) spots; others have

horns as long as a(n) _____ (noun) . Luckily, they seem more interested in eating _____ (noun, plural) than

me! In the distance, I see three cowboys _____ (verb ending in –ing) . Soon their horses are _____ (verb ending in –ing)

and snorting around me. "What in the name of _____ (silly word) is this?" says one. "And what's it wearing?"

says another. I'm wearing my _____ (adjective) sneakers and a(n) _____ (color) _____ (clothing item) . I guess

I look a little _____ (adjective) to them. "Howdy, I'm _____ (nickname) ," I say. "I'm Edwin. This here's

Edmund, and that's Edward," one of them says. "But you can call us Ed." They invite me back to their

ranch to _____ (verb) , so I hitch a ride on the nearest _____ (noun) and follow. Giddyup!

- body part
- verb ending in –ing
- adjective
- verb
- adjective
- noun, plural
- noun
- verb
- noun, plural
- same body part
- noun, plural
- type of appliance
- type of liquid
- noun
- noun
- noun
- adjective

 Fun Fact!

PEOPLE ONCE CLEANED LAUNDRY USING **WASHBOARDS.** NOW THEY'RE USED MAINLY AS **MUSICAL INSTRUMENTS.**

There's a Hole in My Bucket

By the time we get to the ranch, my _____ is _____ from the _____ ride.
(body part) (verb ending in –ing) (adjective)

I'm introduced to the Eds' pa, Egbert, and ma, Edwina, and they invite me to _____ with them.
(verb)

We sit down at a(n) _____ table, where there's a steaming bowl of _____ waiting.
(adjective) (noun, plural)

The cowboys all dig in, but it looks a bit like mystery _____ to me. When dinner's over, the Eds
(noun)

ask me if I want to _____ some _____ with them. But my _____ is
(verb) (noun, plural) (same body part)

still sore from the ride, so I decide to help Edwina wash the _____ instead. I look around for
(noun, plural)

the _____ , but there isn't one! We have to fill buckets with _____ from
(type of appliance) (type of liquid)

a(n) _____ outside. The buckets are as heavy as a(n) _____ , and I think there's
(noun) (noun)

a hole in mine because by the time I get inside, there's hardly any _____ in it!
(noun)

Doing chores at home will be _____ after this!
(adjective)

9

- noun
  - noun, plural
- verb
  - something gooey
- verb
  - type of animal, plural
- noun
  - adjective
- verb ending in –ing
  - verb ending in –ing
- noun
  - adjective
- noun
  - adjective
- verb

Buzzard Blues

That night, I sleep near Ed on a _____ stuffed with _____ . But guess what? Ed
                                   noun   noun, plural

likes to _____ in his sleep! I guess I finally fall asleep, too, because I'm shaken awake a little
             verb

while later. I wipe the _____ from my eyes, and we head out to _____ the
                       something gooey   verb

_____ to new pasture to eat fresher _____ . I saddle up and hop on my very own
type of animal, plural   noun

horse. My horse seems to have its own ideas, though, because it just flashes me the _____ eye
                                                                             adjective

and starts _____ really fast. We're going the wrong way! Suddenly, the horse bucks—and
              verb ending in –ing

next thing I know I'm _____ on a(n) _____ ! Overhead I see a(n) _____
                      verb ending in –ing   noun   adjective

shadow. It's a bird the size of a(n) _____ circling in the sky. A(n) _____ buzzard!
                                          noun   adjective

I'd better _____ before I become buzzard breakfast.
          verb

SOME **SALOONS** DOUBLED AS TOWN MEETING PLACES, OR EVEN AS **COURTHOUSES.**

- type of dessert
  - noun, plural
- animal, plural
  - number
- adjective
  - noun
- noun, plural
  - word beginning with *S*
- verb ending in –ing
  - your favorite color
- type of drink
  - type of game
- noun
  - body part
- noun
  - noun, plural

Dust Bowl

We head to town to get some _____ . The sign at the town's edge says "Dust Bowl," and I can
(type of dessert)

see why! There are _____ everywhere, and more _____ than people. _____
(noun, plural) *(animal, plural)* *(number)*

_____ buildings line the street, including a church, a two-story _____ , and stores
(adjective) *(noun)*

selling _____ . We get thirsty, so we head over to the _____ Saloon. But
(noun, plural) *(word beginning with S)*

when we walk in, everyone stops _____ and stares at me. I walk up to the bar and
(verb ending in –ing)

order a(n) _____ _____ . Some old guys ask if I want to play cards. I'm
(your favorite color) *(type of drink)*

pretty good at _____ —just last week I won my brother's _____ . So I put on my
(type of game) *(noun)*

game _____ and start winning lots of stuff, like a(n) _____ on a chain, a bowler
(body part) *(noun)*

hat, and a "waistcoat," which is basically a shirt without _____ . By the time the game's over,
(noun, plural)

I look a whole lot more like I belong in the Wild West.

13

"COW TOWNS" WERE BUILT AROUND THE CATTLE TRADE. THE MOST FAMOUS WAS DODGE CITY, KANSAS, U.S.A.

- verb ending in –ing
- verb ending in –ing
- clothing item
- color
- noun, plural
- type of animal
- adjective ending in –est
- adjective
- adverb ending in –ly
- noun
- large number
- noun, plural
- verb
- noun, plural
- adjective
- color
- adjective

ROBBERY!

Suddenly, we hear lots of _____ (verb ending in –ing) and _____ (verb ending in –ing) coming from the street.

A man in a black _____ (clothing item) runs out of the bank carrying a big _____ (color) bag

leaking _____ (noun, plural). He jumps onto a _____ (type of animal) and rides off into the sunset. Edwin,

the _____ (adjective ending in –est) brother, gets a(n) _____ (adjective) look on his face. Staring _____ (adverb ending in –ly)

after the rider, he says, "I'm gonna git that _____ (noun)! There's already a reward of _____ (large number)

_____ (noun, plural) for his capture ... and we're gonna _____ (verb) that Dark Rider!" But first things

first—we head over to the dry goods store to get some _____ (noun, plural) for the chase. We load up

on some _____ (adjective) crackers called hardtack, some _____ (color) dried

meat, _____ (adjective) cheese, and a whole bunch of beans!

15

adjective

  verb ending in –ing

adjective

  adjective

noun

  verb ending in –ed

noun

  verb

color

  adverb ending in –ly

verb ending in –ing

  name of a state

color

  adjective

body part

  noun

UP UNTIL THE EARLY 1900s, BARBERS OFTEN DOUBLED AS SURGEONS.

BARBER Shop

HAIR CUT
SHAVE
TRIM
SHAMPOO

HAIRCUT 10 $
SHAVE 5 $
BATH 25 $
SHAMPOO 10 $

The Dark Rider

Wow, this Dark Rider guy sounds _____ (adjective) , so I figure I should know more about

him before _____ (verb ending in –ing) all over the West. The townspeople tell me that the Dark Rider

was once a(n) _____ (adjective) guy who didn't like his _____ (adjective) hair. One day, the Dark Rider

came into town for a(n) _____ (noun) , but the barber _____ (verb ending in –ed) while cutting his hair, and

the Rider was left with more hair on the _____ (noun) than on his head. When the barber made

him _____ (verb) , the Rider went _____ (color) with anger, _____ (adverb ending in –ly) storming

out. He then became a bandit, _____ (verb ending in –ing) banks all over _____ (name of a state) . Now he wears

a(n) _____ (color) wig and a(n) _____ (adjective) bandana on his _____ (body part) to hide

his _____ (noun) . What a hair-raising tale!

- animal, plural
    - adjective
- type of wood
    - type of cloth
- adjective
    - adjective ending in –est
- large number
    - noun, plural
- noun
    - adjective ending in –er
- verb
    - verb
- noun, plural
    - noun
- kind of fruit, plural
    - feeling
- verb ending in –ing
    - adjective

Fun Fact! SOME TEPEES ARE SO LARGE THEY CAN FIT 30 OR 40 PEOPLE INSIDE!

We ride out of town on our _____ , looking to lasso that _____
                          animal, plural   adjective

criminal, but first we stop at an Indian camp to hire a guide. All around the camp are tepees built

of _____ and _____ . They look pretty _____ to live in, so I ask for
   type of wood   type of cloth   adjective

a tour. Inside the _____ one, there are _____ _____ and the
                   adjective ending in –est   large number   noun, plural

biggest _____ I have ever seen! This is way _____ than my room at home!
           noun   adjective ending in –er

Our guide's name is Eagle, and he knows all about how to _____ off the land. Before we go,
                                                              verb

we're invited to _____ with his family. We're given deer meat and _____ , but
                    verb   noun, plural

there's also some tasty _____ on the cob, nuts, and _____ . My parents would
                            noun   kind of fruit, plural

be _____ to see me _____ all this _____ food.
     feeling   verb ending in –ing   adjective

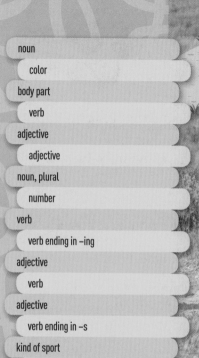

- noun
  - color
- body part
  - verb
- adjective
  - adjective
- noun, plural
  - number
- verb
  - verb ending in –ing
- adjective
  - verb
- adjective
  - verb ending in –s
- kind of sport
  - body part, plural
- verb

Fun Fact! BUFFALO ARE NOT ONLY FAST RUNNERS, THEY CAN ALSO SWIM.

FINISH

Buffalo Buffoonery

We start out on our journey, and soon we're on an endless _____ . There's _____
                                                                    noun   color

stalks of grass as tall as my _____ for as far as I can _____ . But there's something
                                   body part   verb

_____ and brown in the distance. Buffalo! Hundreds of them, just like I saw in the _____
   adjective   adjective

_____ in the library. As we get closer, we notice something odd. Some of the buffalo have
   noun, plural

formed _____ lines. Then they start to _____ at each other. The rest of the buffalo are
          number   verb

_____ around like crazy. Whatever they're doing, it looks _____ , so I decide
verb ending in –ing   adjective

to join in. I get my horse to _____ over to them. They're a lot more _____ up close than
                                 verb   adjective

I thought they would be. Just then one of them _____ at me. Is that an
                                                  verb ending in –s

invitation to play _____ ? I raise my hands and _____ .
                      kind of sport   body part, plural

Get ready to _____ !
                 verb

21

noun

noun, plural

adjective

adjective

noun, plural

noun

noun, plural

silly word

verb ending in –ing

verb ending in –s

famous athlete

verb ending in –ing

adjective

adjective

noun, plural

adjective

Fun Fact! THE "RATTLES" ON A **RATTLESNAKE'S** TAIL ARE CALLED "**BUTTONS.**"

Critters and Cacti

After the buffalo party, we're in a really dry place with the sweltering _____ beating down,
                                                                                      noun

and I'm covered in _____ . It sure is _____ in the sun. There are _____ -looking
                      noun, plural   adjective   adjective

cacti everywhere: the big saguaro that has _____ almost like a tree, the little padded prickly
                                               noun, plural

pear that has edible _____ , and the barrel cactus with its hooked _____ .
                         noun   noun, plural

_____ ! What's that _____ sound? Our guide _____ me on the shoulder, and
silly word   verb ending in –ing   verb ending in –s

I jump higher than _____ . He tells me to stay behind him when we're _____
                       famous athlete   verb ending in –ing

—there are dangers like _____ scorpions, long, _____ rattlesnakes, and brown
                            adjective   adjective

spiders with poisonous _____ . I knew the people in the Wild West could be _____ ,
                           noun, plural   adjective

but not these little critters!

23

ONE OF THE EARLY DEFINITIONS OF "DUDE" WAS A CITY SLICKER WHO HAD TRAVELED TO THE WESTERN FRONTIER.

adjective

verb ending in –ing

type of profession

verb ending in –ed

noun, plural

exotic location

clothing item

noun

type of liquid

noun

snack food

famous city

verb ending in –ed

noun, plural

noun

Pardon Me, Pardner

We come up over a hill and see a(n) _____ train stopped on the train tracks instead
                                        adjective

of _____ through the grassland. There's a(n) _____ in uniform in front,
        verb ending in –ing   type of profession

and he tells us that the Dark Rider has just _____ all their _____ ! Still,
                                                verb ending in –ed   noun, plural

the travelers from _____ seem cheerful. Then a man in a(n) _____ calls to
                        exotic location   clothing item

me: "You there, young _____ , are you here to serve us _____ ?" A woman in
                            noun   type of liquid

a(n) _____ -shaped bonnet asks me to bring her a(n) _____ . These people must be
            noun   snack food

city slickers from _____ back East. Don't they know they've just been _____ ?
                        famous city   verb ending in –ed

Oh well, I think, sticking around long enough to give them _____ . As we ride away, we promise
                                                              noun, plural

we'll catch the _____ who robbed them.
                      noun

adjective

   noun, plural

noun

   verb

something pointy, plural

   noun, plural

verb

   something stinky, plural

something slimy, plural

   noun, plural

noun

   body part, plural

noun

   number

verb ending in –s

   body part

adjective

Fun Fact!

FAMOUS OUTLAW
BILLY THE KID
ESCAPED FROM JAIL BY
CRAWLING UP A CHIMNEY!

Tracking is an art, that's for sure, and these guys are _____ at it. They find little _____
                                                            adjective   noun, plural

everywhere. They can tell if a(n) _____ has been ridden through the grass recently, and where
                                          noun

the Dark Rider stopped to _____ . They get out their _____ from their
                              verb   something pointy, plural

_____ and start to _____ . We find little bits of _____
noun, plural   verb   something stinky, plural

and _____ on the ground. We follow a trail of _____ , but it only leads us
       something slimy, plural   noun, plural

to the side of a(n) _____ . Finally, our guide stops and puts his _____ against
                        noun   body part, plural

a(n) _____ for _____ minute(s) and closes his eyes. I start to wonder if he's fallen asleep
       noun   number

when suddenly he _____ and sticks out his _____ to check the direction of
                verb ending in –s   body part

the wind. Looks like we're back on the _____ trail!
                                         adjective

Fun Fact! A **BUTTE** IS A SMALL, ISOLATED **HILL** WITH STEEP SIDES AND A FLAT TOP.

- color
- verb ending in –ed
- adjective ending in –ed
- body part
- noun
- noun, plural
- type of vehicle
- adjective
- noun
- noun
- noun
- greeting
- same greeting
- silly word
- nonsense word

Grand Greetings

The landscape is getting really wild. The rocks are _____ (color) and curled and _____ (verb ending in –ed) and _____ (adjective ending in –ed). I see formations that look like my dog's _____ (body part)—others are all swirled in different shades of red like an ice cream _____ (noun), some look like ocean _____ (noun, plural), and one is as big as a(n) _____ (type of vehicle). But that's nothing compared to what comes next—the Grand Canyon! Wow, this thing is _____ (adjective) and goes on forever! It must be as deep as _____ (noun). A big _____ (noun) winds its way along the _____ (noun) of the canyon. "_____ (greeting)!" I yell down into the canyon. "_____ (same greeting)," comes the echo back. I try again: "_____ (silly word)," I yell. Only this time, the echo comes back as "_____ (nonsense word)." Who, or what, is down there? I try one last time: "Is anyone there?" "No," comes the reply. *Hmm.*

direction

noun, plural

adjective

feeling

adjective

noun

body part

verb ending in –ing

verb ending in –s

noun, plural

adjective

adjective

adverb ending in –ly

adjective

verb ending in –ing

noun, plural

noun, plural

Tales of Adventure

We head _____ , then stop to ask for _____ from a stagecoach. The driver is
       direction   noun, plural

a(n) _____-looking woman who seems _____ to take a break from the _____
   adjective   feeling   adjective

road. A man with a big _____ under his nose sticks his _____ out the window.
                  noun   body part

We tell him we're _____ after the Dark Rider. He says his name is Mr. Twain. He's a
            verb ending in –ing

writer and also _____ _____ for a living. He likes our story! He tells me I'm a
       verb ending in –s   noun, plural

really _____ kid. I've given Mr. Twain the idea for a(n) _____ novel about a kid on an
     adjective   adjective

adventure! I grin _____ . Then he says that he saw a man a while back on a(n) _____
           adverb ending in –ly   adjective

horse _____ up a big cloud of dust, with big _____ hanging from the saddle,
      verb ending in –ing   noun, plural

like it was carrying heavy _____ . Sounds like it's the Dark Rider!
               noun, plural

noun, plural

noun

noun, plural

noun

noun, plural

noun

noun

adjective

body part

number

verb

something wet

something cold

type of weather

verb

type of animal

verb ending in –ing

Fun Fact!

RIDERS IN THE FAMOUS PONY EXPRESS MAIL SYSTEM WERE MOSTLY TEENAGERS.

We lose the trail of the Dark Rider near the foothills of the _____ . He could be anywhere by
                                                                    noun, plural

now. Just then, we see a(n) _____ racing toward us. It's the mailman! He carries _____
                              noun   noun, plural

in his _____ , and there are _____ hanging from his _____ . That's quite a
         noun   noun, plural   noun

load! He stops and says he can't keep going because he's got a(n) _____ on his _____
                                                                    noun   adjective

_____ . We offer to deliver his packages to the next rider, but they need to be there within
   body part

_____ minute(s)! We take off at top speed, but soon our packages start to _____ and
    number   verb

fall out of the bags. But neither _____ nor _____ nor _____
                                   something wet   something cold   type of weather

can stop the mail from getting through, so we _____ on. By the time we meet up with the next
                                               verb

rider on the _____ Express, he's _____ impatiently and asks what took
              type of animal   verb ending in –ing

us so long. Sheesh! You're welcome!

33

- adjective
- noun
- adverb ending in –ly
- relative's name
- verb ending in –ing
- something shiny
- number
- adjective
- something sticky, plural
- something smelly, plural
- something tasty, plural
- clothing item
- noun
- noun, plural
- verb
- verb ending in –ing
- celebrity's name
- same relative's name

Fun Fact! THE LARGEST GOLD NUGGET EVER FOUND WEIGHED ALMOST 200 POUNDS (91 KG)— ABOUT AS MUCH AS A BABY ELEPHANT!

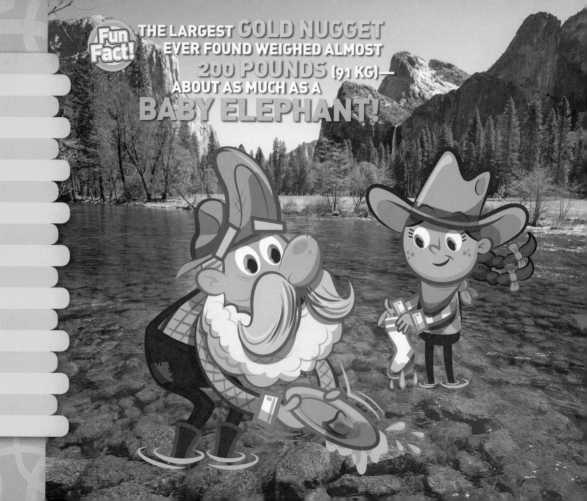

Them Thar Hills

We finally reach some _____ mountains, where a little old man with a big white _____
                        adjective   noun

is _____ leaning over a stream with a pan. His name is _____ , and he's
   adverb ending in –ly   relative's name

been _____ for _____ in these mountains for more than _____
     verb ending in –ing   something shiny   number

year(s). I ask if he has ever found gold, and he says no, but he thinks he's _____ . He tells me he
                                                                              adjective

has found _____ , _____ , and _____ . I decide I want
          something sticky, plural   something smelly, plural   something tasty, plural

to try my luck, but I don't have a pan. So instead, I take off my _____ and use it as a sieve. It
                                                                  clothing item

must be my lucky _____ , because when I check inside, there are lots of little _____
                 noun   noun, plural

in it. I _____ out of the water and see one rock is _____ in the sunlight. Gold!
         verb   verb ending in –ing

I'll be as rich as _____ . Naw, I'll give it to _____ —he deserves it
                   celebrity's name   same relative's name

more than I do.

- noun
  - number
- verb ending in –ing
  - noun, plural
- adjective
  - noun, plural
- noun, plural
  - adverb ending in –ly
- verb ending in –ing
  - adverb ending in –ly
- geometric shape, plural
  - direction
- adjective
  - adverb ending in –ly
- noun
  - noun

Fun Fact! STANDARD TIME WAS ADOPTED IN THE UNITED STATES AND CANADA IN 1883 TO KEEP BETTER TRACK OF TRAIN SCHEDULES.

Mountain Impass-able

We come to a big ravine with a(n) _____ (noun) running through it far below. _____ (number) people are working, _____ (verb ending in –ing) big _____ (noun, plural) to make a railroad bridge. This looks _____ (adjective), so we ask if we can help. We're given _____ (noun, plural) and iron _____ (noun, plural). At first things go _____ (adverb ending in –ly). Then we notice that our track is _____ (verb ending in –ing). And it seems to be going the wrong way! So we _____ (adverb ending in –ly) try to build it the other way, but we just end up going in _____ (geometric shape, plural). Finally, our track is going _____ (direction) again, but we end up right at the side of a mountain! "No problem," says one of the _____ (adjective) workers. He _____ (adverb ending in –ly) stuffs an explosive _____ (noun) into a crack in the rock. *Kablam!* A hole as large as a(n) _____ (noun) appears in the mountain. The guy in charge of the construction doesn't look too happy!

37

- noun
  - noun
- adjective
  - feeling
- number
  - your favorite song
- body part
  - body part, plural
- noun
  - adverb ending in –ly
- verb ending in –ing
  - adjective
- adjective
  - verb
- type of animal, plural
  - verb ending in –ing

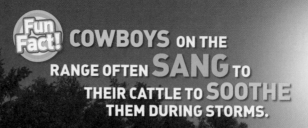

Fun Fact! COWBOYS ON THE RANGE OFTEN SANG TO THEIR CATTLE TO SOOTHE THEM DURING STORMS.

After a hard day's work, we settle down by a big _____ for the night. But just as I'm drifting off
                                                (noun)

to _____ , I hear a(n) _____ cry in the distance. A wolf! At first I'm _____ ,
   (noun)   (adjective)   (feeling)

but then another wolf joins in. And then _____ more. As I listen more closely it starts to sound
                                         (number)

like _____ . I didn't know wolves liked karaoke! I start to clap my _____ and
     (your favorite song)   (body part)

stomp my _____ to the beat. Then I take a big _____ and _____
         (body part, plural)   (noun)   (adverb ending in –ly)

sing out, "I've been _____ on the railroad, all the _____ - _____ day."
                     (verb ending in –ing)   (adjective)   (adjective)

I _____ and wait for applause. There is silence, except for the chirping
  (verb)

of _____ . Then it comes: howls from every direction. We spend
   (type of animal, plural)

the entire night _____ until the sun comes up.
                 (verb ending in –ing)

39

adjective

    adjective

verb

    color

noun, plural

    noun

verb ending in –ing

    verb

adjective

    verb ending in –ing

adverb ending in –ly

    adjective

adjective

    kind of vegetable

verb ending in –s

    noun

your name

Fun Fact! HAIR GROWS AT A RATE OF ABOUT HALF AN INCH (1.3 CM) A MONTH.

Showdown!

In the morning, we awake and head out again. We finally come to a(n) _____ cabin all by itself on
                                                                    adjective

the hillside. The windows are _____ , so we can't _____ inside. We can see that there
                              adjective   *verb*

is _____ smoke rising out of the chimney, and the grass out front is littered with _____ .
   color   *noun, plural*

It sure does look like a place where a dastardly _____ would hide out. We try to sneak up on
                                                 noun

the cabin, but I keep _____ over logs and making twigs _____ . Guess I wasn't
                      verb ending in –ing   *verb*

_____ enough, because the Dark Rider comes _____ out _____ .
adjective   *verb ending in –ing* *adverb ending in –ly*

Things are getting kind of _____ , so I tell the Rider about the time I got a haircut so _____ ,
                           adjective   *adjective*

my hair looked like a(n) _____ . The Rider starts crying and _____ over to give us
                         kind of vegetable   *verb ending in –s*

all a big _____ . _____ saves the day!
          noun   *your name*

adjective

   color

kind of vegetable, plural

   color

type of fruit

   noun

noun, plural

   adjective

noun, plural

   noun, plural

noun, plural

   noun, plural

something found in a bathroom

   something found under your bed

feeling

   verb ending –s

body part, plural

Fun Fact! FAMOUS OUTLAW **JESSE JAMES** HAS BECOME A FOLK HERO, OFTEN COMPARED TO **ROBIN HOOD.**

Heart of Gold

The Dark Rider seems like a(n) _____ (adjective) guy after all. He invites us in for a meal of _____ (color) _____ (kind of vegetable, plural) and _____ (color) _____ (type of fruit) . He thanks us for saving him from being a bad _____ (noun) . Now he's going to return all the _____ (noun, plural) he took from people while he was _____ (adjective) . We saddle up and go out to give back all that _____ (noun) . This guy's been busy! There are gold _____ (noun, plural) , plenty of wedding _____ (noun, plural) , silver and copper _____ (noun, plural) , but also weird stuff like a(n) _____ (something found in a bathroom) and a(n) _____ (something found under your bed) . All the people seem really _____ (feeling) to get their stuff back, and the Dark Rider declares he's going to be a new kind of guy—one who _____ (verb ending –s) instead of steals. The only thing he's stealing now are people's _____ (body part, plural) . *Awww.*

- number
  - adjective
- adjective
  - noun
- geometric shape
  - noun, plural
- adverb ending in –ly
  - noun
- verb
  - noun
- clothing item
  - body part
- same clothing item
  - verb ending in –s
- verb ending in –ing
  - noun

Fun Fact! SQUARE DANCING IS THE OFFICIAL STATE DANCE OF **19 DIFFERENT** U.S. STATES.

HOEDOWN

Happy Hoedown

After _____ day(s) on the _____ trail, we arrive back in town. The
      number   *adjective*

townspeople are _____ to see us and decide to throw a(n) _____ for
           adjective   *noun*

the whole town at the schoolhouse, with a picnic, games, and _____ dancing. It's not a
                                                               geometric shape

big town, but there are lots of _____ to get in on the fun. Kids are _____
                              noun, plural   *adverb ending in –ly*

playing games. I recognize some of the games from back home, like _____ races, marbles,
                                                       noun

hide-and-_____, and jumping _____, but there are other ones like "hunt the
          verb   *noun*

_____." To play, we all sit around in a circle with our knees up to our _____ and
  clothing item   *body part*

secretly pass the _____ to each other while another player _____ for it. This
                  same clothing item   *verb ending in –s*

is some party! I join in the games and the _____, and so does the new town _____,
                                      verb ending in –ing   *noun*

the Dark Rider!

MOST **OUTHOUSES** HAD
TWO HOLES, ONE FOR ADULTS
AND A SMALLER ONE FOR CHILDREN,
SO THEY WOULDN'T **FALL IN!**

verb

verb

type of liquid

adjective

color

verb

adjective

noun, plural

clothing item, plural

adjective

adjective

kind of pet

noun

noun

noun

Chuck Wagon

TODAY'S SPECIAL
**ROOTIN'
TOOTIN'
BEAN
PLATTER**

RESTROOM